*Masonic Symbolism of Easter
and the Christ in Masonry*

By

H. S. Darlington, Joseph H. Fussell,
Joseph Fort Newton and Edgar A. Russell

Copyright © 2020 Lamp of Trismegistus. All rights reserved. No part of this publication may be reproduced or transmitted in any form or by any means, electronic or mechanical, including photocopying, recording, or by any information storage and retrieval system, without permission in writing from Lamp of Trismegistus. Reviewers may quote brief passages.

ISBN: 978-1-63118-434-5

*Foundations of Freemasonry
Series*

Other Books in this Series and Related Titles

A Few Masonic Sermons
by A. C. Ward & Bascom B. Clarke (978-1-63118-435-2)

Royal Arch, Capitular and Cryptic Masonry
by various authors (978-1-63118-425-3)

Masonic Symbolism of King Solomon's Temple
by Albert G. Mackey, David Harlow & Robert Smailes
(978-1-63118-442-0)

Psalms of Solomon by King Solomon (978-1-63118-439-0)

The Two Great Pillars of Boaz and Jachin
by Albert G. Mackey, H. L. Haywood, William Harvey & others
(978-1-63118-433-8)

The Testament of Abraham by Abraham (978-1-63118-441-3)

Masonic Symbolism of the Apron & the Altar
by various authors (978-1-63118-428-4)

Lost Chapters of the Book of Daniel and Related Writings
by Daniel (978-1-63118-417-8)

Cloud Upon the Sanctuary by K. Eckartshausen (978-1-63118-438-3)

Symbolism and Discourses on the Entered Apprentice, Fellowcraft and Master Mason Blue Lodge Degrees by various (978-1-63118-413-0)

The Lost Keys of Freemasonry or The Secret of Hiram Abiff
by Manly P. Hall (978-1-63118-427-7)

The Story and Legend of Hiram Abiff by William Harvey, Manly P. Hall & Albert G. Mackey (978-1-63118-411-6)

Audio Versions are also Available on Audible and iTunes

Table of Contents

Introduction…7

Easter Eggs and Colored Veils
by H. S. Darlington…9

The Significance of Easter: A Masonic Interpretation
by Joseph H. Fussell …19

Acacia Leaves and Easter Lilies
by Joseph Fort Newton…39

The Christ in Masonry
by Edgar A. Russell and Fred B. Leyns …47

Introduction

From the beginning of Modern Freemasonry's birthdate of 1717, the intelligentsia of humanity have found refuge for safe reflection within the walls of the fraternity. Masonic writers have produced a nearly incalculable amount of written musings on a multitude of esoteric and philosophical subjects, as they relate to the ancient mysteries that Freemasonry currently storehouses. Sadly, most of it appears to have sat largely unread, as American Freemasonry in particular, continues to transform itself into something that bears little resemblance to what it was originally designed to be. The true essence of Freemasonry is not that of blind patriotism or a single-minded national religion but one of Universal Brotherhood and altruism, designed for the betterment not just of its members but of society as a whole. In particular, for those who are not members of the fraternity, as Freemasonry has always acted as a beacon, to help guide humanity through darker times, with the hopes that one day we will collectively reach a truly enlightened age.

It's not uncommon for new members joining the fraternity to find little education within the walls of many modern lodges, in spite of so much written material available to the membership. Many older members are not simply uneducated with regards to real Masonic history and symbology, not to mention the vast arena of related subjects, but they are disinterested in all of it, as well.

Lamp of Trismegistus is doing its part to help preserve humanity's Masonic history by making some of these classics available to those students who are seeking to unearth the knowledge of these ancient colossi. As such, Lamp of Trismegistus offers its readers highlights of Masonic study, culled from a variety of authors and viewpoints, with the hope bringing education back into the fraternity. So, be sure to check out other titles in our *Foundations of Freemasonry Series* as well as our *Esoteric Classics*, *Theosophical Classics*, *Occult Fiction* and our *Christian Apocrypha Series*, and don't be afraid to let a little altruism into your own heart or even into your Lodge. You can also download the audio versions of most of these titles from iTunes or Audible, for learning on the go.

Easter Eggs and Colored Veils

By Bro. H. S. Darlington

In a small city, where the writer lived, there is a College, or locus of wisdom, on the eastern edge of town; and on the western edge an abandoned cemetery. How Masonically appropriate this is, that we should find Wisdom or Light's-New-Birth in the East, and that Death, Sunset and Oblivion should be in the West. The College is alive and growing under the care of an excellent Mason; but the old cemetery, as a symbol of mortality, is neglected, forgotten; yes, fairly "overcome".

But just to the east of the College, or rather just to the northeast, as if it were the House of Dawn, there is a spacious lawn belonging to a Mason whose initials are P.A.N. Now this man P.A.N., the wealthiest man in the vicinity, takes a particular delight each Easter Day in inviting the children of the town to hunt out, and roll the various colored Easter eggs that are placed in hiding upon this broad sloping Elysian field. One could almost think the Golden Age of the Greeks was once more upon us.

Masons might well ask themselves: "Is there an appropriate symbolization in this egg-rolling frolic, to the East of the Seat of Wisdom - some spiritual quality or degree of righteousness attainable for man which transcends the Light of Wisdom itself? Is there any significance in the behavior of innocent little children, joyously disporting themselves with brightly decorated eggs, which latter in themselves are symbols of a promise of a New Life - seemingly a Life that shall be gloriously illuminated in the variegated tints of Dawn?"

Before answering our own question, let us give consideration to the most common analogy that mankind observes between himself and the cardinal positions of East and West. From the oldest records that we can trace of ancient philosophies and cultures, and from the information that missionaries and ethnographers have gathered with respect to the more general attitudes of mankind toward the phenomena of sunset and sunrise, we discover that, by far the major number of tribesmen and nations of this earth, have looked upon the setting of the sun in the west as symbolical of the descent of the soul of man into the "underworld" at death. It would appear that the soul or spirit of man is vaguely thought of as being analogous to a luminous something, a sort of glory, that is swallowed up in darkness at death, by the powers of the nether world. With this view, none too well defined, or rationalized upon, in the background of his mind, man has frequently been led, half instinctively, to bury his dead to the west side of his sacred village or hamlet, taking care that the feet should be placed to the east or to sunrise. This custom, however, is by no means absolutely universal.

Accompanying this concept of man's having a soul analogous to the bright sun that sinks unto its death at evening in the west, there has nearly always been the contrasting or reciprocal notion that even as the sun is seen to arise from death in youth and glory, in the rosy east, cleansed from the taints of the underworld by being washed in the baptismal waters of the bright eastern seas, so shall, the soul of man arise ultimately from the grave, in radiance and perfection. And the Day of Resurrection arrives when the Great God Pan shall call the soul out from the underworld of material life, and shall cause it to roll around to the East, where the age-old promise of a new birth shall be fulfilled in the glorious illumination of innocent, sex unconscious spiritual wisdom.

Seemingly, York Rite Masonry is attempting to teach just such a doctrine of rebirth into the very realms of God, when we have gone through the lessons that must be learned in the underworld of death, and materially directed efforts; until at length, by passing through the zone of wisdom, or crossing the college campus, we reach the Elysian Lawns, where we are to disport ourselves in searching out the hidden Egg-of-Rebirth that shall become "our very, very own" when discovered.

Let us pursue an inquiry into the meaning of our rituals. The first three degrees of Freemasonry we may call the illiterate degrees or degrees of *unenlightenment.* We may say of them, to bring out our analogy, that they are the Western, Sunset, or Graveyard degrees because of the blindfolding of the candidate and the plunging of the lodge into darkness, in the third degree. When we say they are the illiterate degrees, we mean that the rites do not assume that the candidate is able to read and write, as the rites in the Chapter do. But the four degrees of the Chapter may well enough be termed the enlightened or literate degrees, the Sunrise, Dawn or Ascension degrees, for the reason is that, learning is looked upon as enlightenment, almost the world over. Even the rude African tribesman, such as the Ekoi, in attempting to divine the future, will hold up an egg to the sun and pray: "As the bush fowl cries for light, so may light be shed on all we wish to know." The Ekoi is looking for more Masonic light in his own way. So, we think, we are justified in asserting that the Chapter Degrees may be termed Eastern, Sunrise or Re-birth degrees.

In the individualistic work of Masonically building a more-stately mansion for his soul, the meditative Mason is searching for that illusive and promissory egg-of-rebirth. He is engaged in the half- drifting, half consciously directed, soul-shaping work of preparing his thoughts and actions by gradually gained spiritual conceptions of man as man, in relation to men, until at length he can tune-in on the harmonies of Deity. In the fourth or Mark Master's Degree, the candidate must be able to read and write, for the first time; for he must be able to read the "marks" or the signatures of the craftsmen, and he must be able to keep time, and figure their wages correctly. In the fifth degree, the candidate attains great wisdom, and is on a par with Solomon, who was the oracle of all knowledge, in the opinion of the ancient Jews. Now, with this attainment of wisdom, he should also attain unto an illumination or unto enlightenment. This idea is accordingly symbolized in the following, the sixth, or Most Excellent Master's Degree. Fire descends from Heaven into the completed Temple. But the Temple, we must ever bear in mind when trying to find out what Masonry means, is invariably the human body, as a housing for the soul. It is intellectual fire that really falls from Heaven. It is, then, spiritual knowledge that is conferred upon the candidate; and thus he becomes transfigured in the sixth stage of soul attainment, and release from the carnal world of matter.

It is not solely the enlightenment of spiritual wisdom that is conferred upon the tyro in this sixth degree; for symbolically, he is freed from all carnal desire, and raised to a level of innocence, and freedom from all shame. This does not mean shamelessness. He is raised to the status of a little child that is naked and innocent and without a sense of shame in his state of unawakened sexuality. This attainment of purity of thought is symbolized by the dropping away of the loin-cloth of shame, which is the apron, in which he was clothed up to the moment of illumination. The real meaning in this connection is not so much that of sexlessness, as it is that of androgyny, or the reunion of the soul that was dichotomized into an Adam half and an Eve half.

The Royal Arch Mason's Degree, or the seventh and last one in the Chapter, comes next. The soul having symbolically been educated and purified in spiritual wisdom and innocence, is in line for the attainment of that status which may be known as Sainthood, Avatarhood, or Christhood. Symbolically taken, this is the approach from the west, eastwardly to the area beyond the campus of spiritual wisdom, even unto the precincts of the Great God Pan; that is to say, the soul advances to godliness in the very realms of God.

However, the seventh degree does not start the candidate off as if he were coming directly from the sixth attainment; but it puts the advancing one through a recapitulation of his whole progress up to that point. He is symbolically put through the first three degrees again, as the first half of the seventh degree. These Blue Lodge degrees are represented in an apparent aimless and discouraging wandering across the desert in an attempt to reach the Holy city. The tyro is blindfolded all this time, because he is supposed to be traversing the Sunset or Unenlightened steps, as prerequisites in soul attainment. Prayers are made, and offerings made at the ancient altars until finally he gets a faint and far-off glimpse of the Holy city of God. Yet, he is left outside of that New Jerusalem, while his spiritual and invisible conductor who has been whispering words of wisdom in his intuitive ear, from time to time, abandons him, and turns him over to a more advanced, brightly robed or illuminated spiritual guide, for further advancement his hoodwink now being removed.

Now his eyes are opened to the non-material world. He finds he is bathed in a glory of lights of varying colors. He passes several veils of different colors, symbolizing a self-radiation of grades of spiritual consciousness. They are supposed to be atmospheres that the candidate sheds about himself by reason of his overcoming material concepts and desires, and an entrance upon spiritual might and effulgence. The total progress is gradual, slow and most discouraging. Each colored veil he passes into symbolizes a new birth in spiritual being, or the finding of another egg-like promise of new, scintillant and vibratory life.

After having been inducted within the first veil, which is really a recapitulation of the fourth or Mark Master's Degree, or is supposed to be, the tyro throws a rod to the ground, which becomes a serpent. This he must pick up by the tail, which is an esoteric way of stating that he must take hold of it in a way that seems to be the reversal of what we would ordinarily call the normal. On so doing, the serpent is immediately transformed into a rod. The lesson in this veil is then supposed to have been mastered by the candidate, who then advances into the second veil.

But this idea of the serpent and the rod cannot be understood in its true psychological import unless we take the psycho-analytical view of it. Following Freud, we may say that the subconscious or the unconscious as we shall call it, does not take either the rod nor the serpent in the literal sense at all. The rod, when held aloft and upright, out of contact with the material ground under our feet, or out of contact with the reproductive soil, or garden of Mother Earth, is a Rod of Command. He who carries this Rod of Command is a sovereign, and a king, by virtue of its mystic properties that may either kill or quicken into life. But, the moment this Rod is thrown down, and plows up this material Mother Earth, then straightway, this Rod of Command is transformed into the lowly "libido." This "libido" is none other than the conscienceless sexual urge, that is said to be so fatal to the gaining of a spiritual consciousness. The serpent is the symbol of the "libido", even of sexuality itself.

The candidate must learn self-control, and suppression of the animal passions. Therefore, he is instructed to pick up the serpent by its tail. In so doing he reverses its nature, so that the libido is lifted into the spiritual plane, and the serpent is sublimated as it were into a Rod of Command over all creation. This sublimation of the "libido" makes man a creator on the mental plane, and a Power and Authority in the Universe, instead of being the slave of carnal desires on the animal plane. Now the spiritual aspirant has done away with sexual desires, in a symbolical way. Thus he has reached the same stage in progress that he symbolically won in the sixth degree when he threw off his loin cloth apron. By rights, this rod and serpent drama should parallel the apron-dropping drama, chronologically, but it does not. This is what we would term a ritualistic error.

When the candidate has advanced to the fourth or last veil, he spills some water on the ground, or rather he discards water for good. Water is a symbol of birth and rebirth, so the psycho-analysts tell us. We see it in the baptismal rites, whereby the child is symbolically and poetically "reborn" into a spiritual life. Hence, in repudiating water, the meaning must be that the candidate is born for the very last time, so that hereafter never again will he need the cleansing offices of rebirth to help him reach the stage of undying, pure, spiritual life. Accordingly, as soon as he spills the water, he is passed out of the last veil and enters into the august presence of the symbolical Trinitarian Deity. All the regalia are now seen to be gorgeous and resplendent, and the tyro himself is clothed in an illuminated robe, and is given a crown to wear. He has now pecked his way out of the last colored egg-shell of clouded comprehension of things spiritual on this symbolical Easter Day . . . the day of his being raised to the Supreme Degree of Royal Arch Mason. Then as a climax to all, a new name, a Trinitarian deific compound, is conferred upon him, thus raising him to companionship with the Highest. The name is a quality of the soul.

York Rite Masonry is really teaching in an esoteric way a doctrine of soul attainment, unto absolute perfection.

Perhaps we can confirm this interpretation of Easter Eggs and Masonry by citing a parallel case from the Bible. When Jesus Christ, who normally was a Rod of Command in the Right Hand of God the Father, according to the Christian tradition, threw Himself down in the Garden of Gethsemane, He met His death and passed down into the Underworld as a Sun that had set. There He stayed for three days, thus symbolizing the three unenlightened degrees of the Blue Lodge. Following that, He was raised from the dead, so that He immediately received a partial enlightenment, such as we try to symbolize in the fourth degree. But He was in a state of only partial corporeality, and He alternated from time to time from a state of visibility to invisibility, still on this earth, over a period of forty days, until His Ascension as a Rod of Command in the Right Hand of His Father. But psycho-analysis informs us that forty days in a psychological sense only means the same as four days, because the Unconscious has no knowledge of noughts in its system of mathematics. Therefore, the three days in Hell, and the forty days on earth, should be added as the sum of three and four, thus making seven. The meanings seem to be that the full period occupied in arising from death to everlasting life requires seven stages of soul growth, of which three are in utter darkness or exclusion of all spiritual light.

Now that Biblical event with spiritual import, that is celebrated in Christian lands on Easter Day, is doctrinally taught by means of dramas in our York Rite Masonry; and moreover, is taught by such beautiful and poetical folk-customs as that very practice at Ada, Oklahoma, where the little innocents find their promised births into perfection, in the diligent but joyous search for their four resplendently lighted sheaths of consciousness, as symbolized in the brightly colored eggs under the radiant smile of the All in All, the Great God Pan.

The Significance of Easter: A Masonic Interpretation

By Joseph H. Fussell

In his volume of verses, under the heading *Portals*, Walt Whitman asks:

"What are those of the known but to ascend and enter the Unknown? And what are those of life but for Death?"

To which, may we not add: And what are those of Death but for Rebirth and Resurrection?

-oOo-

One of the first things brought to the attention of the Entered Apprentice is that no important undertaking should be begun without first invoking the blessing of Deity. The ancient Aryan, as also the devout Hindu today, began and ended every important discourse and undertaking by repeating the Sacred Word. Socrates, in the *Timaeus*, says: "And now, Timaeus, I suppose you are to follow, first offering up a prayer to the god as is customary." To which Timaeus replies:

"All men, Socrates, who have any degree of right feeling do this at the beginning of every enterprise, great or small - they always call upon the gods. And we, too, who are going to discourse of the nature of the universe, whether created or uncreated, if we be not altogether Out of our wits, must invoke and pray the gods and goddesses that

we may say all things in a manner pleasing to them and consistent with ourselves. Let this then be our exhortation to the gods, to which I add an exhortation to myself, that I may set forth this high argument in the manner which will be most intelligible to you, and will most accord with my own intent."

And let me say the same, for there is no higher theme than that which is our subject tonight. It is not only the very heart of the Rose Croix degree, but the heart of Freemasonry, the culmination of all existence, the supreme and last lesson of life.

-oOo-

Every season of the year has its marvel of beauty, its significance. The promise of Spring, the full glory of Summer, the fruitage of Autumn, the rest of Winter: each has something that the others have not, some lesson to teach, some mission to fulfill, some symbol to reveal. Birth, childhood, and youth for Spring, full manhood for Summer, ripe and vigorous old age for Autumn, and death for Winter; each of these is a step on the pathway of Life's infinite journey.

Night is dispelled by day, and day again fades into night; Spring follows Winter, and year succeeds year; so, surely, had we but faith in Universal Law which overrules and guides all, we might know of a certainty that death is not the end of all, but that there is Resurrection, Rebirth; that these are also in accordance with the Law: a new life, and life after life. Is not this one of the lessons of the ever-recurring seasons?

Sweet beyond words to express as is the thought of rest at the close of day, after duty well done; radiant and beautiful as is the angel of death after a life well lived, its soothing hand leaving a happy smile upon the lips; yet neither sleep nor death is the end, each is but a doorway into other realms where we sojourn for a while and then return. This, we know, is true of sleep with its bright dreams, or with its deep dreamlessness from which we awake with no recollection, but with a feeling of perfect happy rest. We do not fear to sleep, nor could any evil dreams trouble us, if the day has been well lived; and so, too, no fear of death can come to one who has lived his life honorably, nobly and well. Why then should it not be with death, twin brother of sleep, that from it too we awake into a new day? It is this, this awakening, this resurrection, that is the message of Easter, it is this that is the heart of the teaching of Freemasonry.

-oOo-

There is a very close connection between the Third or Master's degree, the Eighteenth or Knight Rose Croix, and the Thirty-first; all have reference to Resurrection, which is the great lesson of Easter. It has been said that the Resurrection was the most stupendous event in all history; but when, as Scottish Rite Masons, when, as students of the Ancient Mysteries from which Masonry is descended, we turn to the teachings and traditions of ancient India, Egypt, Greece, and indeed of all the great peoples of Antiquity, we find it not one solitary event, but a recurring event, and thus not less but more stupendous, more inspiring, more significant: the supreme teaching given to all races in all ages.

For each of the great races of the past has had its Savior who taught the people and showed them the true pathway of life. Of many of them the same legends and traditions are told; and many were the "Christs" of pre-Christian ages, said to have been, like Him, born of virgin mothers, and revered as Saviors of men. India had her Krishna, and her Gautama Buddha; China, her Fo-hi and her Yu; Egypt her Horus; Persia had her Zarathustra; Greece, her Apollo and her Dionysus; ancient America her Quetzalcoatl; and many others might be named, all of whom were of divine birth, born of virgin mothers.

And many of the most sacred rites and ceremonies which today are practiced among Christians and by many held to be purely Christian had their origin ages ago among the so-called pagans. Listen to what Rev. Robert Taylor says of the Eleusinian Mysteries (*Diegesis*, p. 212):

> *"The Eleusinian Mysteries, or Sacrament of the Lord's Supper, was the most august of all the Pagan ceremonies celebrated, more especially by the Athenians, every fifth year, in honor of Ceres, the goddess of corn, who, in allegorical language,* had given us her flesh to eat; *as Bacchus, the god of wine, in like sense,* had given us his blood to drink. . . *From these ceremonies is derived the very name attached to our Christian sacraments of the Lord's Supper - ' those holy Mysteries '; - and not one or two, but absolutely all and every one of the observances used in our Christian solemnity. Very many of our forms of expression in that solemnity are precisely the same as those that appertained to the Pagan rite."*

Can we doubt that the ancient Greeks worshiped the true God? Listen to the following Orphic Hymn, quoted by Justin Martyr (*Exhortation*, XV):

> *"Now rather turn the depths of thine own heart*
> *Unto the place where light and knowledge dwell,*
> *Take thou the Word Divine to guide thy steps*
> *And walking well in the straight and certain path,*
> *Look to the One and Universal King –*
> *One, Self-begotten, and the Only One,*
> *Of whom all things and we ourselves are sprung.*
> *All things are open to His piercing gaze,*
> *While He Himself is still invisible,*
> *Present in all His works, though still unseen.*
>
> *And other than the great King there is none.*
> *The clouds for ever settle round His throne*
> *And mortal eyeballs in mere mortal eyes*
> *Are weak, to see Zeus reigning over all.*
>
> *"There is one Zeus, one Sun, one Underworld,*
> *One Dionysus, one lone God in all."*

Or listen to the Hymn of Cleanthes, the Stoic, (Version given by James Freeman Clarke in *Ten Great Religions*):

> *"Greatest of the gods, God with many names,*
> *God ever-ruling, and ruling all things!*
> *Zeus, origin of Nature, governing the universe by law,*
> *All hail! For it is right for mortals to address thee;*
> *For we are thy offspring, and we alone of all*
> *That live and creep on earth have the power of imitative speech.*

Therefore will I praise thee, and hymn forever thy power.
Thee the wide heaven, which surrounds the earth, obeys;
Following where thou wilt, willingly obeying thy law.
Thou holdest at thy service, in thy mighty hands,
The two-edged, flaming, immortal thunderbolt,
Before whose flash all nature trembles.
Thou rulest in the common reason, which goes through all,
And appears mingled in all things, great or small,
Which filling all nature, is king of all existences.
Nor without thee, O Deity, does anything happen in the world,
From the divine ethereal pole to the great ocean,
Except only the evil preferred by the senseless wicked.
But thou also art able to bring to order that which is chaotic,
Giving form to what is formless, and making the discordant friendly
So reducing all variety to unity, and making good out of evil
Thus throughout nature is one great law
Which only the wicked seek to disobey –
Poor fools! who long for happiness,
But will not see nor hear the divine commands.
In frenzy blind they stray away from good,
By thirst of glory tempted, or sordid avarice,
Or pleasures sensual, and joys that pall.
But do thou, O Zeus, all-bestower, cloud- compeller!
Ruler of thunder! guard men from sad error.
Father! dispel the clouds of the soul, and let us follow
The laws of thy great and just reign!
That we may be honored, let us honor thee again,
Chanting thy great deeds, as is proper for mortals.
For nothing can be better for gods or men

Than to adore with hymns the Universal King."

So, too, behind the bewildering array of the divinities of the Egyptian Pantheon we find there also One Absolute Deity, and that the "many gods" do but represent aspects, manifestations, or attributes of that One. That they believed in One God, Divine, Eternal, Infinite, is clearly shown in the following selections from their hymns, quoted by Dr. Alexander Wilder in *Egypt and the Egyptian Dynasties*:

"God is One and Alone, and there is none other with him:
God is the One, the One who has made all things:
God is a Spirit, a hidden Spirit, the Spirit of Spirits.
The Great Spirit of Egypt, the Divine Spirit."

"Unknown is his name in Heaven,
He does not manifest his forms!
Vain are all representations of him."

"He is One only, alone without equal,
Dwelling alone in the holiest of holies."

"He hath neither ministrants nor offerings:
He is not adored in sanctuaries
His abode is not known.
No shrine is found with painted figures,
There is no building that can contain him!"

"God is life and man lives through him alone:
He blows the breath of life into their nostrils."

"He protects the weak against the strong;

God knows those who know Him;
He rewards those who serve Him,
And protects those who follow Him."

And in the so-called *Book of the Dead*, 'The Ritual of the Coming Forth by Day,' we read the following:

"I am Yesterday, ' Witness of Eternity ' is my Name.
"A moment of mine belongeth to you, but my attributes belong lo my own domain.
"I am the Unknown One.
"I am Yesterday and I know tomorrow; for I am born again and again. Mystery of the soul am I.
" 'I who know the Depths' is my Name. I make the cycles of the shining millions of years; and billions are my measurement."

Along with such conceptions of Deity, unsurpassed in any age, is it any wonder that we find the sublimest truths taught regarding Man and Nature, and the supreme truth of all, the divinity and immortality of the soul, and its resurrection? But the ancient Egyptians as well as the Wise Ones of other ancient peoples had a conception regarding the resurrection which is not generally taught today. It is, however, taught in Freemasonry, and particularly in the 3rd degree, though it is not always so interpreted. The conception of the Resurrection usually held among Christian peoples is the one given in the story of the Nazarene, the Great Teacher and Most Wise Master whose name we honor and revere in the Rose Croix, namely, that he suffered for the sins of the whole world, was crucified and was laid in the tomb, and that after three days he rose again, conqueror over death, savior of the world, and that henceforth, through his passion and death, all men who believe in Him, who partake of the Mystic Sacrament of the Eucharist, become one with Him and share in the glory of His resurrection after death.

But so, too, was it taught in the Orphic Mysteries of the Greek Savior, Dionysus, and the Rite of Baptism and the celebration of the Eucharist were essential features of the Greek Mysteries; and the poet Euripides (*Bacchae*, - Murray's translation) thus describes the latter as it was celebrated five hundred years B. C. He is speaking of Dionysus as the Mystic Savior:

> "*In the God's high banquet, when*
> *Gleams the grape-blood, flashed to heaven*
> *To all that liveth His wine he giveth, Griefless, immaculate.*
>
> "*Yea, being God, the blood of Him is set*
> *Before the Gods in sacrifice, that we*
> *For His sake may be blest.*
>
> "*Then in us verily dwells*
> *The God Himself, and speaks the things to be.*
>
> "*The Lord of Many Voices,*
> *Him of mortal mother born,*
> *Him in whom man's heart rejoices,*
> *First in Heaven's sovereignty.*"

And going further back to Egypt; as Marsham Adams declares, in *The House of the Hidden Places*:

> "*We read in the Ritual of an incarnate, and not only of an incarnate, but of a suffering and a dying God. We are confronted*

with the tears of Isis, and with the agony of Osiris - an agony so overwhelming that gods and men and the very devils, says the Ritual, are aghast."

I know not how old is the story of Odin, as told in the Scandinavian *Edda*, perhaps older than that of Osiris. He too though 'Father of the Gods,' 'Divine Wisdom,' 'Creator of men,' suffered and was crucified, and through his sufferings became the 'Savior of mankind.' In Odin's Rune-Song in the *Edda*, Odin himself says:

"I know I hung on a wind-rocked tree, nine whole nights with a spear wound, and to Odin offered - myself to myself - on that tree of which no one knows from what root it springs."

In fact, the story that is told of the Passion and Death and Resurrection of the Nazarene Teacher is the same in its essentials as was told ages earlier of Dionysus-Zagreus, of Osiris, of Krishna and of other Saviors. This story it was that formed the basis of the Mysteries of Antiquity, which in their latest form, as the Isiac Mysteries, existed in Rome side by side with the early Christian teachings for nearly five hundred years, becoming lost, submerged, we might say, only with the advent of the Dark Ages. The same teachings, the same rites and ceremonies and sacraments, the same hope of Resurrection, that are taught and celebrated today in the Christian Church, were taught and celebrated among the Pagans ages before our era. Let me read to you what St. Augustine, one of the early Church Fathers, wrote of the Christian religion; he says (*Augustini Opera*, Vol. I, page 12):

> *"The very thing which is now called the 'Christian' religion, really was known to the ancients, nor was it wanting at any time from the beginnings of the human race up to the time Christ came in the flesh; from which time the true religion,* which had previously existed, *began to be* called *'Christian,' and this in our day is the Christian religion, not as having been wanting in former times, but as having in later times received that name."*

In the 31st degree is given a glimpse of the teachings of the Mysteries of Osiris, the Isiac Mysteries, but only a glimpse is given and it is left to the student to search out their meaning and import. Certain it is that these teachings are among the greatest of the heirlooms that have come down to us through the ages from the very dawn of time. And one of these teachings is that every race and every age has had its Divine Savior who has given his life for the race, for all Humanity.

There is however, as just said, another conception of Resurrection which was taught in all the Ancient Mysteries, and is taught or at least hinted at in Freemasonry, especially in the 3rd degree. It is the supreme goal of Initiation; it is the resurrection, which each must achieve for himself, of the spiritual life, the resurrection of the soul ·while in this life, the attainment of self-knowledge and of the knowledge - not faith nor belief - of immortality. To attain this resurrection there must be a mystical death, there must be the conquest of the passions, there must be a mystical descent into the Underworld, one's own soul must triumph over all the Powers of Darkness, and become one with the 'Father in Heaven.'

Speaking of the 'descent into hell,' H. P. Blavatsky writes that:

"mystically it typified the initiatory rites in the crypts of the Temple, called the Underworld. Bacchus, Herakles, Orpheus, Asklepios and all the other visitors of the crypt, all descended into hell and ascended thence on the third day, *for all were initiates and 'Builders of the lower Temple.'* . . . *To speak, therefore, of anyone having descended into Hades, was equivalent in antiquity to calling him a* full Initiate."

The greatest of all the known Temples of Initiation was the Great Pyramid. It was not built as a tomb for the dead, as were the other Pyramids, but was verily for the dead in life. In the last and highest Initiation after passing successfully all the trials in the various halls and passages, the body of the Candidate lay for three days in the sarcophagus in the King's Chamber while the soul descended into the Underworld to meet the temptations of the Hosts of Darkness and to face Death. If he conquered, then followed Illumination and Resurrection he returned to the outer world as 'a Master of the Royal Secret' to be a teacher and helper of men.

According to Ragon, one of the most learned of the Masons of the last century, our present form of speculative Masonry, and particularly the 3rd degree, is due to Elias Ashmole, the celebrated antiquary and alchemist, and other brothers of a society of Rose Croix in the middle of the seventeenth century, a fact which is of special interest in our present celebration. The methods of initiation, Ragon says, which these Rose Croix brothers then introduced, in place of the ceremonies up to then used by operative masons, were "based upon the ancient Mysteries, upon those of Egypt and Greece." And further on he states that

> *"Ashmole undertook to regenerate, under this architectural veil, the Mysteries of the ancient initiation of India and Egypt, and to give to the new association an aim of union, of fraternity, of perfection, of equality and of science, by means of a* universal bond, *based on the laws of nature and on love of humanity."*

"In Egypt," Ragon declares, "the 3rd degree is named the Gate of Death"; and then after reciting the main points of the ceremonies of this degree, he says:

> *"We recognize, in the modern rite, the reproduction of the Egyptian fable, only instead of taking the name of Osiris, inventor of the arts, or the Sun, the neophyte takes that of Hiram, which signifies* raised, *(an epithet which belongs to the Sun) and who was skillful in the arts."*

-oOo-

The return of Spring is Nature's proof, as the Resurrection of Eastertime is a divine proof that there is no death for the soul. "There is no death; what seems so is transition," says the poet Longfellow. The seed falls into the earth, and soon up springs a flower, or a stalk of wheat, or a tree. Yet the outer form had to die e'er the life-force within could spring upwards into the light. Death always precedes Resurrection.

How beautifully Walt Whitman speaks of Death in his *Song of Myself*. Listen:

"I wish I could translate the hints about the dead young men and women,
And the hints about old men and mothers, and the offspring taken out of their laps.

What do you think has become of the young and old men?
And what do you think has become of the women and children?

They are alive and well somewhere,
The smallest sprout shows there is really no death,

And if ever there was it led forward life, and does not wait at the end to arrest it,
And ceas'd the moment life appear'd."

Truly, what we call death is but a gateway, a transition, a crossing over, an initiation. But Resurrection, as it is taught in Freemasonry, as it was taught in the ancient Mysteries, is something more than a coming to life again, it is something more than what we witness in Nature, wonderful and inspiring as that is. Resurrection in Freemasonry, in the Mysteries, is the Resurrection of the Christos which dwells in the heart of every man, it is a triumph over death, a conquest over Nature, it is the entrance upon Eternal Life. Nature's method is a constant succession of day and night, summer and winter, life and death, reincarnation after reincarnation, until all the lessons of earth-life have been learned. The method and purpose of Initiation, for those who have the strength to undertake the stupendous task, is to learn the lessons *now*; it is, as Paul the Initiate said a "taking of the Kingdom of Heaven by violence"; it is the conquest of one's self, it is the Resurrection of the Divine Spirit of Man.

Consider for a moment what it really means to be a Master Mason. To pass through the degrees gives one the title of Master Mason, but does not constitute one such in reality. Necessary proficiency in ancient times when the Mysteries were enacted in their purity meant more than the possession of a fair memory, it meant more than living a moral life as judged by the standards of the world. To have attained proficiency as E. A. meant, in very truth, that one's passions had been subdued. Proficiency as F. C., meant that one had studied and understood science, philosophy, and art, and had learned to apply these in daily life and conduct; it meant complete control and mastery of the mind. To attain such proficiency in these degrees was not therefore a matter of a few weeks, but of years, perhaps of lifetimes; but when attained then indeed did one become entitled to receive initiation in the 3rd degree, which symbolizes this Resurrection from the tomb, and the recognition and realization of the Divinity that is hidden in the heart of every man.

How is this accomplished in the 3rd degree? You know the reference to the Lion of the Tribe of Judah; but here again we have another proof that the foundation of Masonry is to be looked for in Egypt and India; for in the ancient Mysteries of those lands the same ceremony was enacted by the Lion of Egypt in the one case, and by the Lion of the Punjab in the other. And it should be borne in mind that the Lion as also the Eagle represents the Sun, which again is the emblem of spiritual life, and of the Divine Spirit in the universe and in the heart of man. The Sun is the heart of the Universe, the Lion is emblematic of the power that resides in the Sun, and hence is emblematic of the divine power that resides in the heart of man, and only through that power can man achieve his Resurrection.

-oOo-

This then, I take it, is the Masonic interpretation of the significance of Easter, the significance of the Resurrection, the At-one-ment with Divinity Itself. It is the acquirement of the Royal Secret, the Mystery of the Balance, the Secret of Universal Equilibrium. It is the acquirement of that power by means of which man becomes co-worker with Deity, co-worker with all the great ones of the Past and the Present and throughout all coming ages, - until all Humanity shall indeed become one Universal Brotherhood and so achieve its Divine Destiny.

Is not this one of the most significant teachings of Scottish Rite Freemasonry, in that we thus learn to reverence all who in past ages have been Helpers and Saviors of mankind, learn to see in each of them the manifestation and incarnation of the Deity, appearing under many names in many lands? And of these Great Ones, Walt Whitman speaks m those wonderful lines which he inscribes:

To Him That Was Crucified

"My spirit to yours dear brother,
Do not mind because many sounding your name do not understand you,
I do not sound your name, but I understand you,
I specify you with joy 0 my comrade to salute you, and to salute those who are with you, before and since, and those to come also,

That we all labor together transmitting the same charge and succession.
We few equals indifferent of lands, indifferent of times,
We, enclosers of all continents, all castes, allowers of all theologies,
Compassionaters, perceivers, rapport of men,
We walk silent among disputes and assertions, but reject not the disputers nor anything that is asserted,
We hear the bawling and din, we are reach'd at by divisions, jealousies, recriminations on every side,
They close peremptorily upon us to surround us, my comrade,
Yet we walk unheld, free, the whole earth over, journeying up and down till we make our ineffaceable mark upon time and the diverse eras,
Till we saturate time and eras, that the men and women of races, ages to come, may prove brethren and lovers as we are."

Today we are witnessing events that are appalling in their significance: a World War! Is it the closing of one age and the beginning of another? The old civilization of Europe is in its death struggle. Can it emerge? Is there for us and for the nations of Europe a Resurrection, an Eastertime, a return from the very depths of Hell?

And what part are we playing in this World- Tragedy - we Masons? The Past is past; it is irrevocable; yet the Present is ours, and out of it shall grow the Future. What therefore can we do as Masons; what is the duty and opportunity of the present time? If Freemasonry is heir to the Wisdom of the Ages; if it holds in its keeping the great truths that have been handed down from the days of the Ancient Mysteries - truths that are for the healing of the Nations and the guidance of the people; if indeed we have a knowledge of these truths, are we not called upon as Masons to herald a Resurrection, an Easter time such as the world has never yet seen, a Resurrection of the Spirit of Brotherhood which has suffered death and lain so long in the tomb?

That, I think, is the message of this Eastertime; that, I think, is the challenge of the Christos to us Masons today - to see to it that the Masonry which we profess is not a dead letter, but a living power. And if we make the Spirit of Masonry, which is the Spirit of Brotherhood, a living reality in our own lives, we shall make it also a living reality in the life of Humanity; so great, I verily believe, is the potential power in our Masonic Fraternity. For true Brotherhood is not alone for the few, not alone for the Initiated, but for all Humanity.

Events are moving so rapidly, the times are so crucial, we cannot remain passive. Either Freemasonry must become an active factor in this Resurrection or be left a derelict, a lifeless ritual from which the soul has fled.

Never before has Freemasonry had such a glorious opportunity as it has today. The Christos Spirit is waiting to be born anew in the life of Humanity; it is pleading with us to do our part, and if we will but do our part in the Resurrection which must take place, first in the life of each of us, then, truly, truly, the Christos Spirit shall be born again in the life of all Humanity.

As Robert Browning makes Paracelsus say:

> *"'Tis time*
> *New hopes should animate the world, new light*
> *Should dawn from new revealing to a race*
> *Weighed down so long, forgotten so long."*

That new hopes will animate the world; that new light will dawn, that a new revealing of the Truth has been made, I, for one, feel assured. What part will Freemasonry play in the new Resurrection?

Acacia Leaves and Easter Lilies

By Joseph Fort Newton

April brings us to Easter Day - the festival of Memory and Hope. That a day in spring should be set apart in praise of the victory of Life is in accord with the fitness of things, as if the seasons of the soul were akin to the season of the year. It unites faith with life; it links the fresh buds of spring with the ancient pieties of the heart. It finds in Nature, with its rhythm of winter and summer, a ritual of hope and joy.

So run the records of all times. Older than our era, Easter has been a day of feast and song in all lands and among all peoples. By a certain instinct man has found in the seasons a symbol of his faith, the blossoming of his spirit attuned to the wonder of the awakening of the earth from the white death of winter. A deep chord in him answers to the ever-renewed resurrection of Nature, and that instinct is more to be trusted than all philosophy. For in Nature there is no death, but only living and living again.

Something in the stir of spring, in the reviving earth, in the tide of life overflowing the world, in the rebirth of the flowers, begets an unconscious, involuntary renewal of faith in the heart of man, refreshing his hope. So he looks into the face of each new spring with a heart strangely glad, and strangely sad too, touched by tender memories of springs gone by never to return, softened by thoughts of "those who answer not, however we may call."

Truly, it is a day of Hope and Courage in the heart of man. Hope and Courage we have for the affairs of daily life; but here is a Hope that leaps beyond the borders of the world, and a Courage that faces eternity. For that Easter stands, in its history, its music, its returning miracle of spring - for the putting off of the tyranny of time, the terror of the grave, and the triumph of the flesh, and the putting on of immortality. Men can work with a brave heart and endure many ills if he feels that the good he strives for here, and never quite attains, will be won elsewhere.

There is something heroic, something magnificent in the refusal of a man to let death have the last word. Time out of mind, as far back as we can trace human thought - in sign or symbol - man has refused to think of the grave as the coffin lid of a dull and mindless world descending upon him at last. It was so in Egypt five thousand years ago, and is so today. At the gates of the tomb he defies the Shadow he cannot escape, and asserts the worth of his soul and its high destiny. Surely this mighty faith is its own best proof and prophecy, since man is a part of Nature, and what is deepest in him is what nature has taught him to hope.

For some of us Easter has other meanings than those dug up from the folklore of olden time. Think how you will of the lovely and heroic figure of Jesus, it is none the less His day, dedicated to the pathos of His Passion and the wonder of His

Personality. For some of us His Life of Love is the one everlasting romance in this hard, old world, and its ineffable tenderness seems to blend naturally with the thrill of springtime, when the finger of God is pointing to the new birth of the earth. No Brother will deny us the joy of weaving Easter lilies with Acacia leaves, in celebration of a common hope.

The legend of Hiram and the life of Jesus tell us the same truth; one in fiction and the other in fact. Both tragedies are alike profoundly simple, complete and heartbreaking - each a symbol not only of the victory of man over death, but of his triumph over the stupidity and horror of evil in himself and in the world. In all the old mythologies, the winter comes because the ruffian forces of the world strike down and slay the gentle spirit of summer; and this dark tragedy is reflected in the life of man - making a mystery no mortal can solve, save as he sees it with courage and hope.

Jesus was put to death between two thieves outside the city gate. The Master Builder was stricken down in the hour of His Glory, His Prayer choked in His Own Blood. Lincoln was shot on Good Friday, just as the temple of Unity and Liberty was about to be dedicated. Each was the victim of sinister, cunning, brutal, evil force - here is the tragedy of our race, repeated in every age and land, as appalling as it is universal, and no man can fathom its mystery.

Yet, strangely enough, the very shadow which seems to destroy faith, and make it seem futile and pitiful, is the fact which created the high, heroic faith of humanity, and keeps it alive. Love, crucified by Hate; high character slain by low cunning! Death victorious over life - man refuses to accept that as the final meaning of the world. He demands justice in the name of God and his own soul. The Master Builder is betrayed and slain; his enemies are put to death - that satisfies the sense of justice. Jesus dies with a prayer of forgiveness on His lips; Judas makes away with himself - and the hurt is partly healed.

But is that all? On the mount of Crucificiton, by the outworking of events, goodness and wickedness met the same muddy fate - is that the meaning of the world? The Master Builder and his slayers are alike buried - is that the end? Are we to think that Jesus and Judas sleep in the same dust, all values erased, all issues settled in the great silence? In the name of reason it cannot be true, else chaos were the crown of cosmos, and mud more mighty than mind!

When man, by his insight and affirmation of his soul, holds it true, despite all seeming contradiction, that virtue is victorious over brutal evil, and Life is Lord of Death, and that the soul is as eternal as the moral order in which it lives, the heart of the race has found the truth. Argument is unnecessary; the great soul of the world we call God is just. Here is the basis of all religion and the background of all philosophy. From the verdict of the senses and the logic of the mind, man appeals to the justice of God, and finds peace.

Thou wilt not leave us in the dust:
Thou maddest man, he knows not why-
He thinks he was not made to die;
And thou has made him: thou art just.

With what overwhelming impressiveness this faith is set forth in the greatest Degree of Freemasonry, the full meaning and depth of which we have not yet begun to fathom, much less realize. Edwin Booth was right when he said that the Third degree of Masonry is the profoundest, the simplest, the most heart-gripping tragedy known among men. Where else are all the elements of tragedy more perfectly blended in a scene which shakes the heart and makes it stand still? It is pathetic, It is confounding. Everything seems shattered and lost. Yet, somehow, we are not dismayed by it, because we are made to feel that there is a Beyond - the victim is rather set free from life than deprived of it.

Without faith in the future, where the tangled tragedies of this world are made straight, and its weary woe is healed, despair would be our fate. By this faith men live and endure in spite of ills. Its roots go deeper than argument, deeper than dogma, deeper than reason, as deep as infancy and old age, as deep as love and faith - older than history - that the power which weaves in silence, robes of white for the lilies or red for the rose, will the much more clothe our spirits with a moral beauty that shall never fade.

But there is a still deeper meaning in the Third Degree of Masonry, if we have eyes to see and ears to hear. It is not explained in the lectures; it is hardly hinted at in the lodge. Yet it is as clear as day, if we have insight. The Degree ends not in a memorial, but in the manifestation of the Eternal Life. Raised from the dead level to a living perpendicular by the strong grip of faith, the Master Builder lives by the power of an endless life. That is to say, Masonry symbolically initiates us into Eternal Life here and now, makes us citizens of eternity in time and bids us live and act accordingly. Here is the deepest secret Masonry has to teach - that we are immortal here and now; that death is nothing to the soul; that eternity is today.

When shall we become that which we are? When shall we, who are sons of the Most High, born of His Love and Power, made in His Image, and endowed with His Deathless Life, discover who we are, whence we came, and whither we tend, and live a free, joyous, triumphant life which belongs of right to immortal spirits! Give a man an hour to live, and you put him in a cage. Extend it to a day, and he is freer. Give him a year, and he moves in larger orbit and makes his plans. Let him know that he is a citizen of an eternal world, and he is free indeed, a master of life and time and death - a Master Mason.

Thus Acacia leaves and Easter lilies unite to give us the hint, if not the key to a higher heroism and cheer, even "the glory of going on and still to be;" a glory which puts new meaning and value into these our days and years - so brief at their longest, so broken at their best, their achievements so transient, and so quickly forgotten. Sorrows come, and heartache, and loneliness unutterable, when those we love fall into the great white sleep; but the sprig of Acacia will grow in our hearts, if we cultivate it, watering it the while with our tears, and at last it will be not a symbol but a sacrament in the house of our pilgrimage.

>*What to you is Shadow,*
>*to Him is Day,*
>*And the end He Knoweth;*
>*Thy spirit goeth;*
>*The steps of Faith*
>*Fall on a seeming void,*
>*and find A rock beneath.*

The Christ in Masonry

By Edgar A. Russell
and Fred B. Leyns

*"When Righteousness
Declines, O Bharata l When Wickedness
Is strong. I rise from age to age and take
Visible shape, and move a man with men,
Succoring the good, thrusting the evil back
And setting Virtue on her seat again."*
        -Song Celestial, Arnold.

Recent commentary in the Masonic press carries the intimation that some writers are endeavoring to Christianize Masonry. From the comments and the context we presume that the brethren meant trying to conform Masonry to the specific limitations of some creed. Now we agree that this attempt, if indeed it is being made, would result in nothing but confusion, because Masonry teaches men to: "Be of that religion in which all men agree; that is to be good men and true, or men of honor and honesty, whereby Masonry becomes the center of Union and the means of conciliating true friendship among those that must have remained at a perpetual distance." Creeds are matters of belief and beliefs separate men; and most often the cleavage comes along the line of a nonessential. But there is a body of knowledge that unifies men; and it has been known to some in all ages and climes, including this present age and clime, through the experience of "Initiation," or the discovery of The Christ within—"That Light which lighteth every man that cometh into the world." The Christ Principle is in Masonry and a little study will disclose it under many veils. From the

Ancient Sun Myth of Egypt, which is the basic form, it may be traced down the ages, from the Mysteries in which this myth was developed and purified for a chosen few, to the narrative of the life and experiences of Jesus of Nazareth, where it was still further developed and purified for the many. With the advent of the Nazarene, the Sun of God became the Son of God, prefigured in the Sun Myth. This Son, or Emanation of the Principle of Light, Life and Love, became The Christ—The Messiah—The Redeemer of the World. In the Egyptian and in later mysteries, the candidate was placed in a death-like sleep, during which the Ego was liberated from the physical body, and made acquainted in the spiritual realms with mighty truths concerning the spiritual basis of the universe, and the real nature of "life" and "death."

This statement is neither more nor less than an explanation and a parallel of experiences mentioned in both the Old and New Testaments. After being *raised* to consciousness again in the physical body, this knowledge remained and constituted an "Initiation." The candidate had in fact, by the assistance of the powers of the Hierophant, *travelled in foreign countries.* Those students in this age who approach the altar of Truth divested of prejudice and invested with toleration, may glean many hints from the religious lore of other lands, notably India; but the greatest occult book ever given to man is the Holy Bible, and we may find therein landmarks concerning this matter of "Initiation." Running through its pages, appearing and disappearing like a thread of gold in a tapestry, there are gleams of a *metallic* kind. Let us follow the clue. Hiram, the Master Builder, was the *son of a widow*. Elijah, afterwards reincarnated as John the Baptist, is represented as raising the *son of a widow.* Jesus of Nazareth, the Greatest Master of whom we know, raised at Nain the *son of a widow.* Perhaps the whole story is told in the Bible narratives, perhaps not. The Bible makes no secret of the fact that Jesus had esoteric instructions for his disciples. It is a fair question, therefore, were these two raisings in fact Initiations? The landmark is there and it forms a cable tow between the Old Testament and the New. In both cases it was the *son of a widow* that was raised. "He that is able to receive it, let him receive it." The Legend of the Builder is one of the variations of this same Story of the Ages, the old, old story of the effort of man to know himself, to know his God, and to find the way whereby At-One-ment might be effected; for At-One-ment is something more than Initiation; it is the attainment of the stature of a Master. We shall understand this Legend of the Builder if we study it in the light which preceding degrees shed upon it. Divorced from this introductory work it ceases to teach what it is intended to teach. Studied as history alone, it becomes meaningless and leads to confusion worse confounded. The Legend as we have it today is an evergreen Acacia concealing the place where a mighty truth is buried. This Truth-this open secret of the ages— is the fact that those worthy and well qualified may, by personal study and effort, and the subduing of the lower nature, bring about the personal experience of Initiation, or the discovery of The Christ within. It is possible to attain to an individual experience of the Rising of the Star in the East, a personal knowledge of the birth of the Christ Child in the heart, and a personal responsibility for its nurture in the Manger, and its development in grace and truth. It is significant that the Child is laid in a Manger which is a place where Beasts are fed. This, because the Child must take the place in the heart formerly occupied by the "beasts," or the passions and desires of the lower nature. We say growth and development advisedly, for this experience of Initiation is not accomplished all at once. It is attained by effort and in progressive stages. There is an old saying, "The Adept becomes, he is not made." It is something like this: at just the right time, a man grasps the real beauty and significance of one of those beams of the Spiritual Sun that are being poured out on us all continually, and it leaves him no peace until by effort and development he becomes worthy of receiving more light.

At no time in the history of the world has a vital interest in these things been more necessary than now, when men are adrift from their old moorings.

The current interest in the more sensational aspect of psychic and occult possibilities is but the floating branches which betoken the approach of land.

In the Legend of the Builder, Masonry presents a Constructive Allegory reflecting this evolution of the human soul, and such allegory most certainly goes back to the *remotest ages of antiquity*.

In no age of the world has the Father left his Children without light. Always there has been a body of men highly advanced in spiritual truths. The modern title of Master Mason is only the reflection of a great reality, a reality that inspires, teaches and directs from behind the scenes. It is the reality hinted at in the lecture on the Apron, in the words, "Except he be a *Mason*." There is indeed a small band. "Many are called and but few are chosen." Their ranks are open to all on the sole test of merit, or *proficiency in the preceding degrees*. Scattered inconspicuously about the world in many differing races and climes, they are referred to, broadly speaking, as The Masters; and the more advanced, tried and tested of the fellowcraft sometimes find the way to their doors.

An Ancient Legend in which this spiritual truth of the evolution of The Christ in man is told under the guise of a narrative of physical events, divides naturally into three periods. In a way, these periods may be spoken of as Initiation, Probation and Enlightenment.

INITIATION

The great event of this first period is an experience through which the candidate obtains a brief glimpse of the true Light. Henceforth he *knows* that there is Light to be had and where to seek for more.

Almost his first desire is to share this knowledge with a brother; but he is restrained by a tie stronger than human hands can impose. He cannot *give* this light to another.

He can, if that other is ready, lead him to a place of preparation where he will find out how to attain this light for himself.

So we see that the main lessons of this first period are the attainment of initial light, the assumption of an obligation, and the understanding that the Path of Attainment must be trodden, each for himself in the silence of his own soul.

One reason why we see so much in print about the lesser psychic phenomena and so little about the genuine higher experiences (and there are such) is hinted at by A. P. Sinnett in his "Esoteric Buddhism," where he says: "The Neophyte no sooner forced his way into the region of mystery, than he was bound over into the most inviolable secrecy as to everything connected with his entrance and further progress there. the chela or pupil of occultism, no sooner became a chela, than he ceased to be a witness on behalf of the reality of occult knowledge." That is, as we understand the passage to apply today, he at least ceases to be a witness as to times, places, or persons connected with his own novitiate or even the fact that he is a novice.

There is another landmark connected with this first period, and mentioned by the Nazarene, and that is that he who would tread this path must resolve to "lay up for himself treasures where neither moth nor rust corrupt," treasures that *last, something of a metallic kind.*

PROBATION

The second period is one of testing and may cover a long lapse of time. It may have to do with a great deal of study or a great deal of purification, or both, depending upon the personality of the candidate.

He is made acquainted with an extension of his responsibilities, commensurate with the new opportunities afforded him; and it is at this stage that there is brought particularly to his attention the Legend of the Middle Chamber, one of the most beautiful pieces of symbolism in the esoteric work; and one which cannot too strongly be commended to the consideration of the student. The Neophyte is informed that he must come into touch with a certain "Master," in a place called the "Middle Chamber," where he will receive further instructions. The story runs that this Chamber is approached by an ancient winding stair having Three, Five and Seven Steps. Where and what Chamber? Do you know of any more ancient Middle Chamber than the human brain —middle in function— between body and spirit? Is there anything more winding than its physical convolutions, or anything more twisted and involved than the webs of sophistry it can spin when reason refuses to be guided by Love? Is it not in truth the very place where Jesus said to seek for the Kingdom of God within ? Perchance it is the Shrine where true Knights may still find and drink of Life from the Holy Grail. As to the numbers Three, Five and Seven, it would be hard to pick out any having more symbolic meanings associated with them, and we only note a few in passing. The number Three may refer to the Trinity of

God, Man, and the Means which establishes their Mutual Relationship, whereby the Three that can always hold a Master's Lodge are manifest. As to the Five, the Five Pointed Star is an ancient geometric glyph of Man. Man with his head erect and hands and feet outspread and exhibiting the Five Points of Fellowship. We have no doubt whatever that the Seven, in this connection refers to the Seven Stations of the Cross which we must all pass on the way to self-mastery. In another way, this is the Seven Principles of man which must be brought is this Middle under control by the Ego in order to complete its evolution on this planet. These Seven Principles are symbolized in the Apron, where we have the Four Lower principles, represented by the Square, supporting the Three Higher principles, represented by the Triangle; and the Triangle is folded down into the Square, indicating that the work of the Divine Triad in Man is to inform, vivify and spiritualize the Four Lower principles, which constitute the Four Square Foundation Stone of the New Jerusalem.

ENLIGHTENMENT

Of the Third Period, little can be said to him who has been raised from the Dead Level to the Living Perpendicular, or from the grave of materiality to the Living Plumb, which expresses the integrity of Unity or At-One-ment with the Father of Lights or the Sun of God. But the Legend runs that the Plumb must be tested and proved by the Angle of a Square. Now the Angle of a Square is the *essential element* of a Cross, because the right angle indicates the greatest possible divergence between two straight lines; and is therefore a symbol of the fundamental conflict between Human Desire and Divine Will within the Mind of Man—or the Passion of the Cross. Hence we may say that the Neophyte is *proved by* the Cross and is *raised on* the Cross, for when the Level is raised to the Plumb the Cross is *demonstrated*. The Human Mind is the theater wherein this Mystery of Initiation— this Passion of the Cross is accomplished. • In this Third Period, the Middle Chamber now consecrated by long and pure worship, has become the Sanctum Sanctorum or Holy of Holies, or the Most Retired Apartment of the Mind. In that place, where the Soul communes with the Over Soul—in *perfect silence*—and thus receives that Wisdom and Strength requisite to meet the text, the obligation is recognized and assumed; Gethsemane is experienced; the Cross is taken up; Calvary is ascended and Golgotha is endured. We may not carry this further. Those who can appreciate the real significance of the land mark, *sons of the widow*, a significance that we have only hinted at, will know where to look for Initiation, and how Man is raised from the

Cross of Matter. They will know who speaks in making the promise: "He that liveth and believeth in me shall never die."

They will know how to answer the question,—"What shall we do with the body?"—the body of Truth that lies concealed under the accumulations of the Temple.

www.ingramcontent.com/pod-product-compliance
Lightning Source LLC
LaVergne TN
LVHW041500070426
835507LV00009B/706